Let's Go Cruizin' Again

REMEMBERING MORE NORTH COUNTY "HAPPY DAYS"

1950S - 1970S • FEATURING FLORISSANT, FERGUSON & HIGH SCHOOL MEMORIES

Lets Go Cruizin' Again
By Craig Kaintz with Bill Kasalko

Copyright © 2011 by Craig Kaintz with Bill Kasalko

ISBN: 978-1-891442-74-2
$22.95

Library of Congress Control Number: pending

All rights reserved. No part of this book may be reproduced in any form or by any electronic or mechanical means, including information storage or retrieval systems, without permission in writing from Virginia Publishing Co., except by a reviewer, who may quote brief passages in review.

Designed by Ben Pierce and Kate Huffman
Copy editor: Steve MacDonough

Printed in the United States of America

Virginia Publishing Co., St. Louis, Missouri, 63108.
www.CruizinNorthCounty.com

CONTENTS

Introduction...5

I. "Be True to Your School" - High School Memories...................7

II. "Apple, Peaches, Pumpkin Pie" - Great Food......................31

III. "Home Cookin'" - Tasty Recipes.......................................57

IV. Big Screen - Popular Drive-Ins and Theaters.....................67

V. "Papa's Got a Brand New Bag" - Favorite Stores and Malls....73

VI. "It's All in the Game" - Games We Played.........................85

VII. "I Get Around" - Cruizin' Kids..95

VIII. "Fun, Fun, Fun" - Fun Places.......................................99

IX. "Pleasant Valley Sunday" - Churches..............................113

X. "Paperback Writer" - Authors...117

XI. "R-E-S-P-E-C-T - Acknowledgements and Photo Credits....121

We dedicate our book to everyone who
shares the memories and spirit of North County.

INTRODUCTION

Who knew cruizin' is still so popular? Your response to our *Cruizin' North County* book, the 1950s to the 1970s, was remarkable with over 6,000 sold. At book signings, high school class reunions, and TV and radio appearances we reminisced with you about the special places we featured, but you wanted more.

So, *Let's Go Cruizin' Again!* Our new book includes more North County Happy Days from the 1950s to the 1970s, featuring Florissant, and Ferguson.

It features more hangouts, movie theaters, drive-ins, bowling alleys, skating rinks, 5&10s and other cool places. How about dancing at the Castaway Club; a movie at the Janet, 270 Drive-In or Village Square; bowling at Dick Weber Lanes; roller skating at Hodges; or taking your date to Mr. Yac's, LaRocca's or the 94th Aero Squadron? Did you hang out at Green Lea after school, cruize through Chuck-A-Burger in Ferguson, share a pizza at Pirrone's or Faraci's, have a cone at Velvet Freeze or a malt at Howard Johnson's? Penny candy? You had to go to Nagle's, Ben Franklin or Paul's Market, and you probably picked out some new threads at the Ferguson Department Store, Britt's or Robert Hall.

To top it off, *Let's Go Cruizin' Again!* has North County high school memories including mascots, dances, proms, bands, sporting events and special memories. Our book even includes special recipes from many popular restaurants!

Sit back and cruize one more time with your family and friends.

Hey, do you remember when...?

I. "BE TRUE TO YOUR SCHOOL"

High School Memories

Berkeley High School

Opened in 1937 on Walter Avenue in Berkeley; home of the Bulldogs.

Memories...

The Bells of Berkley

Some creative students decided to do some "maintenance" on the school's bells. One by one, they removed the bell's metal covers. Result: no one knew when to change classes. Temporary mayhem – then busted.

Laugh Out Loud

Comedian Cedric the Entertainer (Cedric Kyles) was a well-known 1982 Berkeley grad.

New Bulldog House

Berkeley closed in 2003 to make way for the expansion of Lambert International Airport. All Berkeley students moved to the new McCluer South Berkeley High School.

Corpus Christi High School

Opened in 1957 on Switzer Avenue in Jennings; home of the Crusaders. The school was co-ed until it became an all-girls school in 1966. Corpus closed in 1973.

Memories...

Strike!
There was a four-lane bowling alley in the basement of the gym, and Kam's Cottage was a popular hang-out for the students. How about a chocolate or cherry coke? Clarence Orthwein, a popular janitor at Corpus, was a frequent visitor to the alleys.

Lights, Camera, Action!
James Grumich, the English/drama teacher, directed over 100 plays at Corpus Christi. It was not uncommon to have four plays a year. When the train passed on the tracks next to the Old Hall, the actors were directed to stop until it passed. However, one night as the train could be heard in the distance, a creative actor who was playing a drunk staggered to window and yelled, 'Tell Casey Jones hello!'

Hideaway
A very slim student was convinced by his friends to skip class and hide out inside a classroom podium. A few minutes after Fr. Voelker started teaching religion class the podium started moving across the front of the classroom. The double take on the good Father's face was a classic! The students broke out in laughter but the young boy did not get the last laugh. He was off to the principal's office.

Fairview High School

Opened in 1926 on Emma Avenue in Jennings and home of the Blue Jays until ithe mascot was changed to the Warrior in 1957. Fairview merged with Jennings High School in 1969.

Memories...

Cookies?
What better way to show Fairview sportsmanship than the Fairview girls serving cookies to the opposing team after the varsity basketball games.

Parallel Parking
Snowy day, classes are kind of boring, so how about moving Mr. Cooper's small car? A group of brawny students picked up his car and moved it sideways next to the sidewalk, taking up two spaces. Trapped! The look on his face – priceless! What's next: Mr. Cooper again, with the pins removed from his classroom door. When he walked in, he began 'dancing' with the heavy door!

Look Out!
Mr. McCracken was teaching his class about gravity by dropping some items on the floor. He had to leave the room and told the class to continue. Bad move! The students began throwing books, pencils, you-name-it out the window. He returned just in time to stop the typewriter from taking flight!

Ferguson High School

Opened in 1939 on January Avenue in Ferguson; home of the Comets. Ferguson annexed the Florissant School District in 1952. In 1962, Ferguson/Florissant became McCluer Senior High School.

Memories

Bull's-eye!
There was a firing range in the basement of Fairview High School used for target practice by students in the NRA Club.

Timber!
Taking class pranks to a new level. In the spring of 1958, three students cut down one of two huge Mississippi Cypress trees on the Fairview campus. The young lads, one of whom had worked for a tree surgeon during the summer, were severely punished. They slept nights in jail, worked under guard during the day cutting up the tree and were expelled from school.

Jackxxx!

Donkey basketball games were the rage in the 1950's through the 1970's and beyond for some schools. Players would ride donkeys up and down the court and take shots. At Ferguson, it could be the teachers versus the students, or the classes playing each other. It was commonplace to see the players pulling the stubborn donkeys down the court. The donkeys just forgot to call a time out. Think of the lnes the students used while watching their favorite teacher ride a donkey!

Hazelwood Central High School

Opened in 1954 on New Halls Ferry in Florissant; home of the Hawks.

Memories...

Bottoms Up!
A flagpole with no flag? Opportunity! Some Hazelwood students coerced a fellow student, who was small in stature, to be hoisted part way up the flagpole by tying the rope to his feet. It was quite a sight to see him dangling upside-down. After a quick salute, he was grounded.

Playmate of the Year
Yes, Patti McGuire, a 1977 Hazelwood grad.

Mission Impossible!
A 'creative' group of students left a window open in the Biology Lab and at 2 a.m., after the janitors left, made their entry. They went through the window, into an AC duct and made it to the principal's office. Lookouts were posted in several places with walkie-talkies to monitor the patrol cars. Everyone was dressed in black with darkened faces – like Navy Seals. With the master key in hand, they opened the doors of numerous students' lockers and moved books from floor to floor, wing to wing. The key was returned, and under cover of darkness they escaped the way they entered. No one was ever caught, but during graduation someone rang a bell for each culprit when they received their diploma.

Hazelwood East High School

Opened in 1975 on Dunn Road; home of the Spartans.

Memories...

Got Your Goat!
The 'goat path' led from the school property to a commuter parking lot. Hazelwood students would sometimes make a quick exit from campus to grab a smoke or cut class.

Hey, Be Quiet!
When Hazelwood East was built, the classrooms had portable, movable walls, but they didn't quite live up to their billing. You could easily hear what was going on in the next room. They were all eventually replaced by permanent walls.

Forks and Spoons!
Piece by piece, a group of Hazelwood girls smuggled forks and spoons from the cafeteria in their purses and stashed them in an empty locker. As the school year came to an end, an anonymous tipster let the assistant principal know about the caper. As the locker was opened, there was a waterfall of silverware! The good news: no punishment for the pranksters.

Hazelwood West High School

Opened in 1975 on Howdershell Road in Hazelwood; home of the Wildcats.

Memories...

Black Tie!
Why would students be dressed in tuxedos at school functions and serve as greeters, attendants and valets? They were part of the Hazelwood West Visitor Information Personnel (VIPs). VIPs for events held early in the day wore white gloves and red jackets.

Bustin' at the Seams
As building construction was being completed, more than 10 classes were held at the same time in one area of the school and some classes were held in rooms where the walls were not yet completed.

Incarnate Word Academy

Opened in 1932 on Normandy Drive in Bel Nor; home of the Red Knights.

Memories...

Tradition

Every year there is a special event at Incarnate Word: the Rose and Candle Ceremony. Speeches are given by the four senior girls who were class presidents. The juniors present roses to the seniors and the seniors give candles to the juniors, thus passing on the 'light of leadership.'

Baby It's Cold Outside

A caring IW student thought the dummy in Sr. Reparata's biology class was chilled with the winter weather, so she put her madras jacket (remember madras?) on it. She didn't see it for a week and was afraid to tell anyone. The good sister made her 'sweat' a bit.

Popcorn from Heaven

In the late 1950s, a couple of fun-loving students decided to liven up the quiet library. Late in the evening, they snuck in the library and filled the bowl-shaped light fixtures with popping kernels. During the first period in library, it didn't take long before, to the Sisters' amazement, popping noises were followed by popcorn from heaven. Salt, anyone?

Jennings High School

Opened in 1912 on Cozens Avenue in Jennings, it was home to the Bulldogs until it merged with Fairview and they adopted the Warrior.

Memories...

Bringing History Alive
John 'Jack' Maier was a popular history teacher. He would liven up his classes by dressing up as famous historical figures. He was also well known for driving his Model T to school.

Class of '64?
A few seniors decided to leave their mark on their soon-to-be alma mater by climbing to the chimney above the library and painting a big, black '64' on each side of it. The bad news is the hard earned class money, normally used to improve the campus, had to be used to sandblast the numbers off of the chimney. The ironic part of this prank is that the story was shared by Rick Perry, who is currently the Director of Public Works for the City of Jennings. Wonder how he knew the details?

AN ERA ENDS
A NEW EPOCH BEGINS

Kinloch

Opened in 1936 on Witt Street; home of the Braves. Kinloch closed in 1976 and the students moved to McCluer North High School.

Memories...

History

The original Kinloch High School was renamed Berkeley High School, which opened in 1937. A new Kinloch High School was opened in 1938.

Last Laugh

Oliver Dillingham, a popular Kinloch teacher, was born and raised in Arkansas. Some of the students used to razz him about his Arkansas accent and roots. One of these students came into his classroom and asked him if he saw an article in the 'Ebunny' magazine. Oliver responded 'Ebunny! What is that'? The student went to the library, brought the magazine back only to have Oliver get the last laugh. 'Son', Oliver said, 'that's Ebony not Ebunny! If his embarrassment wasn't bad enough, the student was given a new nickname, Ebunny!

Champs

Kinloch's basketball team won the 2A Regional Championship in 1974.

Lutheran North High School

Opened in 1946 on Waterman and moved to their current Lucas and Hunt location in 1965. It was known as Lutheran High School and Lutheran Central in its previous locations, and was the home of the Crusaders.

Memories...

Omm Pah Pah

Lutheran North had a German band that performed the Fall Festival in the 1963-64 school year. The band members were part of the overall school band.

Dressed for Success

The administration decided to relax the dress code in 1972 and leave it to the students' discretion. Looked good on paper. In 1973 strict guidelines were established, no cutoffs, shorts, short dresses or play clothes.

Things Were Hopping!

It was early one morning when a few students snuck into the gym with some live cargo. It didn't take long for them to release hundreds of grasshoppers, which took off in every direction across the gym floor as the students made a quick exit, confident that morning chapel would be disrupted. But wait, a maintenance man came to the rescue with his vacuum, quickly sucking all of the bugs up. Chapel started on time - the Lord provides!

McCluer

Opened in 1962 on South New Florissant; home of the Comets.

Memories...

Big, Bigger
In 1971, McCluer had more than 4,500 students even though the school was built to handle 3,300. To handle the extra students, there were two sessions every day, with class beginning at 6:45 and ending at 5:30.

Watch Where You Walk!
Students, faculty and staff never stepped on the 'Crest Seal' on McCluer's Building M-3's floor. It you were caught, you had to kneel down and kiss the seal or maybe take a shot from an upper classman. It was donated by the McCluer's first graduating class of 1963.

Oh McDonald!
Singer Michael McDonald was a McCluer student. Besides his success as a solo performer, he is known for performing with 'Steely Dan' and 'The Doobie Brothers'. His St. Louis bands included 'The Guild', 'Mike and the Majestics' and 'Jerry and the Sheratons'. Michael left before graduating but was named an 'honorary graduate'.

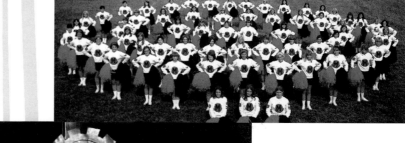

McCluer North

Opened in 1971 on Waterford, Florissant; home of the Stars.

Memories...

Overexposed!
During a baseball game on campus, a car pulled up on the right field side on St. Catherine and from left field came some of the soccer team's finest – STREAKING! Oh, my!

Floor It!
Calm day at school in 1975? No. With doors held open on each end of the Commons, a brave McCluer student rode his dirt bike right through the school.

Ow, What Was That?
A future engineering student decided to spice up a varsity basketball game. The opponent was Riverview. He rigged a slingshot up his arm under his jacket and launched BBs at the Riverview players. After a few strikes, the game was stopped and the authorities came into the stands. In an effort to ditch the evidence, he spilled a box of BBs through the metal stands and onto the floor – BUSTED!

Normandy

Opened in 1923 on St. Charles Rock Road; home of the Vikings.

Memories...

Skinny Dippin'!
With a pool on campus, the boys swam nude until the mid '70s. A belly flop could change the vocal range permanently. The girls swam in oversized, and sometimes torn, school-issued swimsuits.

Smokin'!
Students were allowed to stop for a smoke between classes, but only along 'smoke walk' between the cafeteria and East Hall, while the teachers puffed away in their lounges. Popular hangouts in the neighborhood were Deters Gas Station and To Jo's Market.

Happy Holidays!
Normandy's select vocal group, the Rhythmaires, relished several mornings off from school during the Christmas holidays when they went to Lambert Airport to sing carols to bewildered travelers. More musical talents – Normandy's marching band directed by Herb D. was nationally known. They performed on the Muny stage in The Music Man.

Pattonville

Opened in 1935 on St. Charles Rock Road then moved to Creve Coeur Mill Road; home of the Pirates.

Memories...

Competitors!
Pattonville and Ritenour regularly exchanged class pranks. The Pattonville students would cover up the 'leg' of the big R on the side of Ritenour's football field to form a P. Ritenour would return the favor by adding a 'leg' to the Pattonville's P on their field using white field chalk.

Road Rage!
A group of 'fun-loving' seniors met at the Venture lot before school and formed a convoy on McKelvey Road moving toward the school at a snail's pace. The principal received several calls about the convoy from irate motorists. He returned the favor by having the maintenance staff block two of the exits after school, thus sending a message to the seniors and other students. As the students slowly left the parking lot, the principal and assistant principal stopped each car for a safety belt check.

Up on the Roof!
It was a cool rainy night with homecoming the next day. After a few cold ones, a buddy suggested putting Coach Linn's Volkswagen on top of the press box. How cool would it be the next morning when the students, faculty and staff saw the car? The word got out and 25 football players, using a chain and muscles, pulled the car up the steps. It almost slipped a few times but they finally 'made the mountain top.' It was a sight to behold the next day, and though the coach was a little upset that he could never prove who did it – we think he knew. Here's to the class of '76!

Prep North

Opened in 1965 on St. Catherine in Florissant; home of the Crusaders.

Memories...

A Squeaker!
Math class could get boring sometimes. What better way to liven it up than to have one of the guys bring his baby sister's squeak toy? The students would pass it around the class, causing the squeak to come from different directions. The teacher could never quite figure out what caused the noise as he turned around with a puzzled look on his face. However, the class got a kick out of it!

1 - 2 - 3!
Remember when you had to try different sports during gym class? In an effort to spice up the wrestling class, a few students turned it into Wrestling At The Chase with moves of Dick the Bruiser, Cowboy Bob Ellis, Lou Thez and others. The gym teacher did not remember teaching the sleeper hold, reverse rolling cradle, back breaker, or the iron claw.

No Class!
How to make history at Prep North? Try creating the first yearbook to be condemned by the administration. The 1975 yearbook contained unflattering caricatures of the faculty, missing classmate pictures of females and Colonel Sanders, a student who was an Alfred E. student look alike, and yearbook patrons such as Friar Tuck, Semore Hiney and Bette Wetter.

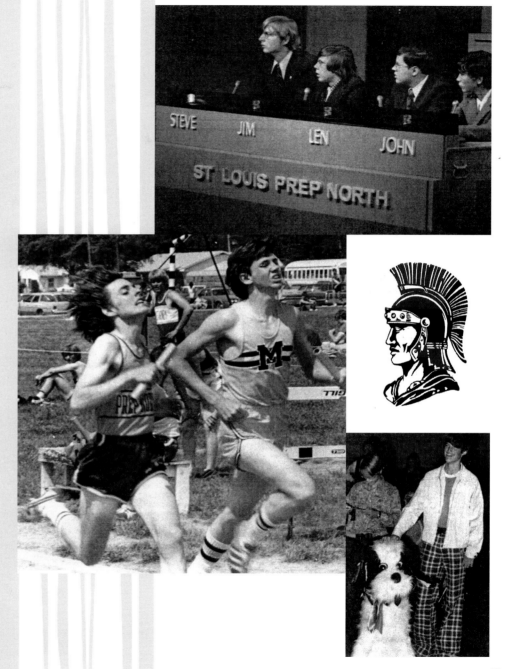

Ritenour

Opened in 1911 on St. Charles Rock Road; home of the Husky's.

Memories...

Soppin' Wet!
Some students learned the hard way that not locking your locker is a bad move. Some Ritenour pranksters took all of the gym clothes out of the unlocked lockers, soaked them in the shower, and 'politely' placed them back in the lockers — and locked them of course! Although the coach thought he knew who did it, he could never prove it and no one was punished.

Fire!
A student and member of the 'Untouchables' group of pranksters borrowed a dime from a friend and, from the phone booth outside the principal's office, called the Overland Fire Department to report a fire in the principal's office. He was still there when the firemen arrived, directing them to the principal's office. What's even worse is that he did it a couple times before they realized the calls were coming from inside the school.

Wanna Have a Good Time?
The Untouchables decided to let some buddies know that there were some wild girls at a remote farmhouse having a party. Two cars of guys pulled up to the farmhouse and a couple of the pranksters from the first car approached the door. A large man emerged from the side of the house and unloaded a 16 gauge shotgun! They dropped to the ground and the man shouted obscenities, firing more rounds into the air. The other car of guys sped away, went to the house where other friends were having a party, and told them the first car pranksters was shot and left for dead! Panic and shock set in until the pranksters arrived at the party totally intact. Gotcha!

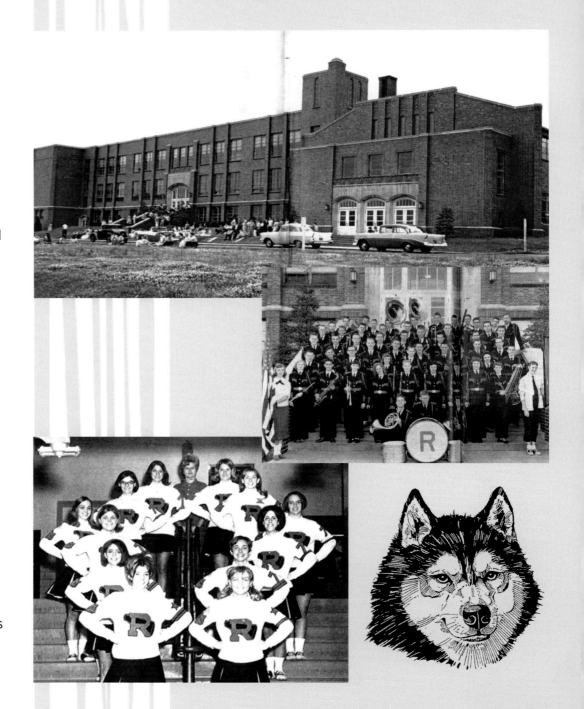

Riverview

Opened in 1927 on Shepley Drive; home of the Rams. Bob Kuban graduated from Riverview in 1958.

Memories...

In Memory
Riverview's football field was dedicated in 1955 to the first Riverview Gardens alumnus to die in Vietnam, Dale Meyercord.

Friday Night Lights
In 1966, football coach Gerald Nordman arranged to purchase the old Busch Stadium lights from Gussie Busch when the stadium on Grand and Dodier closed. The football players from the classes of 1967 and '68 dug trenches and holes for the installation between summer football practices. In September 1966, Riverview played their first home game under the lights. The Rams were 8 and 1 that year and 9 and 0 the next year, winning the state title. Dan McDonough '68, a member of those teams, believes the player's hard work inspired their victories. To date, no other Ram's football team has been undefeated.

Tired?
A group from the class of 1984 decided to leave their mark. They hauled about 75 tires to the football field and spelled out an '8' and a '4' on either side of the 'RG'. Okay, who's going to haul them away??

Rosary

Opened in 1961 on Redman Road; home of the Rebels. Rosary became Trinity Catholic High School in 2003 with the Aquinas/Mercy merger.

Memories...

Lookout!
Where did the Rosary girls gather to have a smoke? The girl's restroom, of course, but not without having a designated look out posted outside the door to watch for the good sisters. All went well until one day when a girl's hair caught on fire. Busted!

Scissorhands!
Father McClain ran a tight ship at Rosary. What did he enjoy doing every year on the first day of class? Going to each freshman homeroom and looking for young men with long hair. If it was hanging too long on their forehead, he would cut a V with his scissors. The next day it was short.

Reaching New Heights!
The girls at Rosary had to be ready for a surprise skirt measurement by the good sisters. If you were singled out for your 'mini skirt' you had to stand up straight with your arms by your sides. If your skirt was shorter than your fingertips, you were sent home – not good! Solution, the girls, who normally had their skirts rolled up at the waistband, would unroll them before the measurement - good to go! (At other girl's schools, there was a supply of old, long skirts - and the girls were given the 'pleasure' of wearing one. And, even if the girls did not have their skirts rolled up during the day, after school in the parking lot - rollin, rollin!)

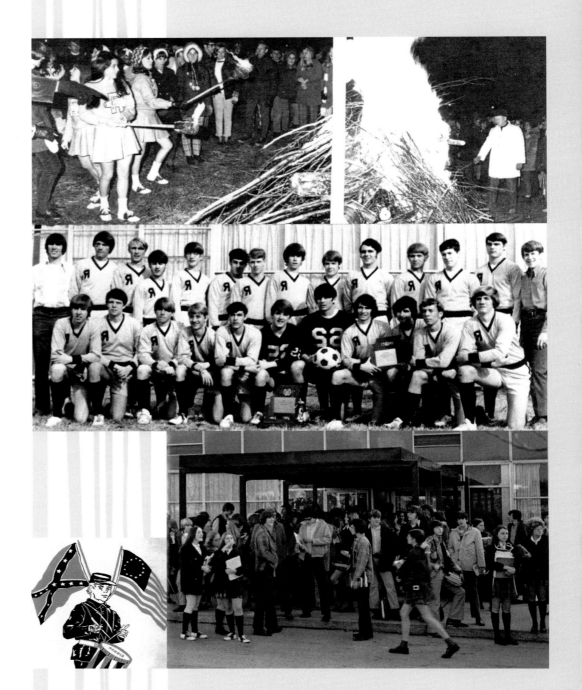

St. Thomas Aquinas

Opened initially as 9th grade class in 1954; moved to the Dunn Road campus as St. Thomas Aquinas High School in 1956; home of the Falcons.

Memories...

Snow Job!
Who doesn't like a snow day? A few enterprising Aquinas seniors met a school at 1:00 a.m. on a snowy winter night and shoveled huge piles of snow against the front and rear school doors. Would it be enough to cancel classes? No – only the first two classes were cancelled. The entire student body had to endure the cold while a maintenance worker shoveled the snow away.

Just Barely
In the spring of 1976, an unnamed senior boy embraced the 'streaking' fad during class one day. An accomplice drove him to the area between the two classroom buildings, and he got out wearing only a paper bag with holes cut out for the eyes. He casually walked toward the building doors and encountered one of the school nuns. No less than 112 classrooms were facing his performance. After a brief face-to-bag confrontation, the student turned and walked back to his get-away car and rode off into the lore of Aquinas High School. He was never officially identified (it's not the kind of lineup anyone would want to witness), but everyone eventually knew who it was.

Green Green Grass
Sometime in the early '80s, a very patient group of seniors showed up one winter night at Aquinas armed only with flashlights and grass fertilizer. They spelled out a brief critical comment about the school's current principal in the grass with the fertilizer and waited a couple of months for Mother Nature to be their accomplice. When the grass on Pep Rally Hill came alive in early spring, the fertilizer did its job and the message appeared in the darkened lush grass like it had been written with disappearing ink. When the principal learned of the message, maintenance was sent to mow the hillside, but the fertilized grass held its color for quite a while.

Wellston (Halter and Eskridge)

Opened in 1906 on Sutter Avenue; home of the Trojans. It had three locations prior to Sutter Avenue. Wellston is now part of the Normandy School District.

Memories...

Cookies to go!
Whenever the home economics class would bake cookies, the basketball team would quickly walk by the class and grab the cookies from the rack. How to stop these thefts? The next batch was chock full of Ex-Lax. Unfortunately, there was a big game later that day. 'Coach, I'll be right back!'

Dance the Night Away
There are many fond memories of the Sadie Hawkins, Sweetheart, Jingle Bell Hop and 'Welhisco' dances.

Kegger
Wellston and Normandy High School, football rivals, played annually to claim the 'Wooden Keg'!

What were some of the Cruizin' hot spots in North County?

Steak 'n Shake on West Florissant, Lindbergh, New Halls Ferry, Natural Bridge, and 'the one and only' Circle Steak.

Totes 'Big Boy' on West Florissant, Lindbergh and Natural Bridge.

The Rock Road, North Florissant Road and Lindbergh Chuck-a-Burgers, and McDonald's on 367, Lindbergh, Halls Ferry, and Parker Road.

Jack in the Box on Halls Ferry, and Dunn Road at Washington.

Burger King on Lindbergh.

It was also fun to park in front of the Rock House on West Florissant, across from Velvet Freeze, and see who was cruizin' by.

II. "Apple, Peaches, Pumpkin Pie"

Great Food

Chuck-A-Burger

In Ferguson — Another great cruizin' spot in the heart of Ferguson, with car hops ready to serve those fantastic burgers! Check out the poodle skirts on the car hops at the Chuck-A-Burger on St. Charles Rock Road. Cruize to the Chuck-A-Burger on the Rock Road for a classic burger.

Howard Johnson's

A favorite North County restaurant, HoJo's had great ice cream, shakes and sundaes. Also known for their all-you-can-eat specials. Our group of guys was asked on more than one occasion to leave after we had chowed down on too many plates of fried chicken!

TOTES BIG BOY

With locations on the Halls Ferry Circle, West Florissant, Lindbergh and Natural Bridge, the chubby boy in the red-and-white-checked overalls held up their double-decker cheeseburger. Totes pioneered the double-decker burger with two patties on a three-layer sesame bun with lettuce, a slice of cheese and the special Big Boy sauce.

Green Lea

Fran and Matt's place on Florissant and Airport Roads opened in 1952. Green Lea featured hand-dipped ice cream (5 cents a scoop!), homemade candy, great burgers, milk shakes and fries. The burgers had to be big enough to hang over the bun. It was the 'Happy Days' place to be before Richie Cunningham and the Fonz ever appeared. The jukebox had all of the latest hits and the pinball machines were always clanging away. It was a popular hang out for students from Ferguson, De-Andries, Incarnate Word, Aquinas and other schools. After Green Lea, it became Milo's. Matt passed away in 1979 but Fran is still active, with her children Mark, John, Tom, Michael and Linda in Russo's Catering and Spazio's Westport. Fran was honored by the Ferguson Class of 1955 for all she did for the students and the area. Russo's on Page has excellent catered meals and dine-in selections. Spazio's is a popular venue for wedding receptions, rehearsal dinners, reunions, banquets and meetings. Stop by and see Fran or Mark. www.russosgourmet.com

Grone's Cafeteria

A fixture in St. Louis, Grone Cafeteria was opened in 1931 by George Grone on the corner of South Grand and Lafayette. Dave Grone, whose great-grandfather was Louis, worked in the business for a brief time at the Grand location and the Woodson Terrace location, which opened in 1969. The family opened a location in Webster Groves in 1986. Both locations closed in 1986, but the memories of the excellent food and friendly service remain. Gone's was known for their family recipes: egg custard pie, sauerbraten, coleslaw, German potato salad and pineapple upside down cake. Their pies were so popular that often there were 30 in the oven at the same time. Dave had other successful careers after Grone's closed but continues to hear from old customers and staff.

Chicken King

North County is well known for its chicken restaurants, and one is still going strong after 50 years – the King reigns supreme! Chicken King, located in Riverview Plaza, 8933 Riverview Drive, is still cooking its trademark chicken dinners and party wings as well as seafood dinners and tasty sandwiches. Chicken King was a frequent stop when we grew up in North County. Service is still fast and the chicken delicious. When I was dating my wife, my father-in-law frequently sent me on a 'run' to Chicken King. We recently stopped by Chicken King; it tastes the very same! Stop by and see Dorman, the owner, for some excellent chicken. Pictured is the mural as it appears on the restaurant wall today.

Velvet Freeze

Who didn't go to a Velvet Freeze for their favorite flavor? Was it mint chip, gold coast chocolate or vanilla? Remember their malts, shakes, banana splits and Wonderdogs? What about the signs showing the 'Teen Time Limit'? We used to frequent the Velvet Freeze in the Riverview Plaza. Once, there were over 90 locations in the Midwest but the only remaining one is in North County at 7355 West Florissant. The original recipe ice cream is made at this location and all of the flavors still taste great! Stop by and see Barbara and John to bring back your childhood memories. They are open Wednesday through Sunday.

Fritz's Frozen Custard

Once an A&W, Fritz's Florissant location opened in 1983. Our children loved going to Fritz's for a cone, sundae or their famous Turtle! You can now find Fritz's Frozen Custard in St. Peters, West County, O'Fallon and Wentzville. Stop by any of their locations for great custard.
www.fritzsfrozencustard.com

Old Town Donuts

The best donuts! Old Town has been in business since 1968, moving to its current location on New Florissant Road in Old Town Florissant in 1980. Owner Keith Took has a passion for donuts as evidenced by his 2009 award from WIL-FM – #1 donut shop in metropolitan St. Louis. KSDK also featured Old Town as a top-ranked place people would visit one more time if they were leaving the area. Stop by and see Keith and his team for a chocolate long john, glazed, old fashioned or one of many other varieties.
www.oldtowndonuts.com

94th Aero Squadron

An aviation-themed country French restaurant right by the Lambert Field runways. Many romantics became engaged or attended a prom dinner at the 94th Aero Squadron. It was cool to watch the planes land and take off almost right in front of you, especially the F-15s. Their photographs, artifacts and replicas were intriguing, and you could even listen to the control tower. It opened in 1973 and closed in 2003 due to runway expansion.

LaRocca's

A memorable Italian restaurant on New Halls Ferry close to Parker. Tom and Dan LaRocca's place was known for pasta, steaks, seafood and chicken spedini. Many dishes were prepared table-side. After dinner, a nightcap could be enjoyed in the Pompeii Lounge. Many local politicians and businessmen were regulars at LaRocca's. It was also a popular place for wedding receptions and rehearsal dinners. Pictures include the grand opening led by Mayor Eagan with Tom and Dan on either side of their maitre d'. LaRocca's was open from 1971 to 1982; it then became Jordan's Restaurant.

Cusumano's

If you are from Glasgow Village, went to Riverview High or anywhere else in North County, you will remember Cusumano's. Cusumano's was opened by John and Bobbi Cusumano in 1972. They had some experience, as both worked at Cusie's on Jenning's Road, which was owned by John's mother. Cusumano's was so popular, they expanded their space in 1978. The pizza and other Italian dishes are great – all homemade. It was a popular place to take your date or grab something to eat after a game. In the summer of 2008, Julie and Chris Walsh opened Cusumano's in O'Fallon on Technology Drive, which recently became Angelo's Chicago Taste. Angelo's specializes in Chicago style Italian food but will continue to serve Cusumano's thin crust pizza. Stop by and bring back those memories of Glasgow Village with family and friends.

Rizzo's

A favorite North County Italian restaurant to which to take your date, celebrate special occasions or gather with family and friends. Rizzo's is located on Dunn Road in Florissant. Excellent pasta, chicken, seafood and pizza – you can even create your own. Specialty dishes include chicken and beef spedini and chicken modiga. Rizzo's is also known for their specialty desserts and affordable lunch specials. Visit them for delicious Italian cuisine. www.rizzosflorissant.com

Burger Chef

There were several Burger Chefs in North County. Known for those tasty charbroiled burgers, fries and shakes. The sauce on their burgers was a combination of ketchup and tartar sauce, so we understand. Remember getting your burger 'with' or 'without' the 'works bar'?

Pirrone's Pizzeria

A long-standing popular Florissant restaurant known for their St. Louis-style pizza, they also serve salads, chicken and fish dishes. Great place to take the family, friends or a date. Pirrone's can also accommodate events or private parties. Before moving to Pirrone's Plaza on Washington Street, they were around the corner. Stop by for some excellent pizza.
www.pirronespizza.com

Yacovelli's

One of the oldest restaurant families in St. Louis, Yacovelli's was founded in 1919 by John Yacovelli. In 1952, Dewey Yacovelli originated the idea of a salad bar. Yacovelli's came to North County in 1966, moving to the current building in 1977 when Jack and Jan opened Mr. Yac's. We went to Mr.Yac's countless times when we were dating, always enjoying the salad bar and excellent food. Yacovelli's continues to be a popular place for wedding receptions, rehearsal dinners, business meetings, family gatherings and special events. More recently, Yacovelli's dinner specials, such as prime rib on Tuesdays, have been very successful. They specialize in steaks, pasta, chicken, homemade crab rangoon and toasted ravioli. Pictured are the bar in Yacovelli's first North County location, the grand opening at Dunn Road, which was in front of Mr.Yac's (Marie and Jan Yacovelli, Mayor Eagan, Jack and Dewey Yacovelli), a portrait of Jan and Jack and Yacovelli's today. Visit Yacovelli's for fantastic food and service! www.yacovellis.com

Note: Years ago Yac's used to be an A&P store. Other stores included Wedge Variety Dime Store and a drugstore with a soda fountain. You could get a five-cent cherry coke in a paper cup with a metal cup holder, and the ice cubes were tubular.

White Barn

For 30 years, the White Barn has been serving indescribably 'addictive' half-pound hamburgers – so big they take about 15 minutes to cook! Located on Chambers Road, just west of Hwy. 67/ Lewis and Clark in Moline Acres (and their second location in Florissant, 2182 N. Lindbergh), the White Barn burger will challenge your jaw - but what the heck, go ahead and try the triple burger! Rich Robson, also known as Dick the Diner, was the original owner but is now the head chef, as Debbie and Ed Mueller own the restaurant. 'The Barn' has a great selection of sodas and other special dishes including pork steaks and sausage, and they buy their food products from local producers whenever possible. Don't let the modest exterior fool you; stop by 'The Barn', drive up, get in line and get ready to enjoy a great burger at a North County landmark. The White Barn puts other burger places to shame!

Ruiz Mexican Restaurant

In 1966, Jose Ruiz married Hortensia Santacruz. As a result of their love for Mexican food, they convinced the owner of Roy's Tavern in rural Florissant to allow them to serve their excellent food in a corner of his establishment. It was known as La Cocina Mexicana, and while most people were not familiar with Mexican food, it did not take long for the word to get out that Florissant had landed a treasure. Lines developed every night including many McDonnell Douglas employees who had moved to, or were visiting St. Louis from their southern California location. Jose was the "ultimate host," working each table after cooking the delicious dishes for his guests.

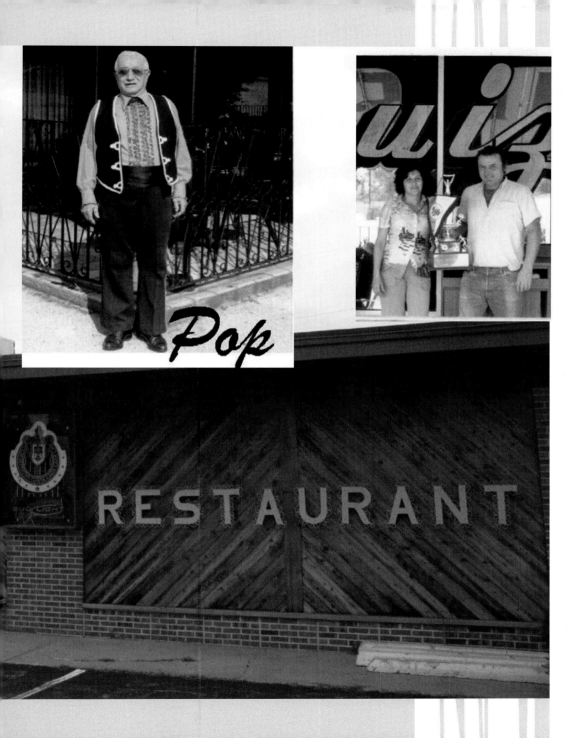

The success story of Ruiz was just beginning. Six months after La Cocina Mexicana became Ruiz, they moved to the current site but occupied only one of eight units in the building. In 1986, the restaurant was turned over to their daughter and son-in-law, Marisa and Doug Marshall. Now occupying all eight units, Ruiz continues to serve excellent Mexican cuisine, always featuring new dishes. The fourth generation of the family is now involved in running the restaurant. They have numerous 'regulars' from Florissant and all over the St. Louis area, but they welcome everyone to enjoy their hospitality. Pictured are Pop - Jose Santacruz, Tencha (Hortensia Santacruz), and Jose Ruiz, Ruiz Mexican Restaurant as it appeared in the '70s and today's Ruiz – stop by for great Mexican cuisine.
www.dineruiz.com

Luigi's/Meglio's Italian Grill & Bar

When we were cruizin' teenagers, Luigi's was the standard by which good pizza was judged. In 1923, Angelina Guislaniani and Antonio Meglio married and in 1953 opened the first of several Luigis'. Our favorite location was on Natural Bridge opening in the late '50s. It was the place to go after a movie, dance or any occasion. Grandma Angelina taught young John Meglio her secret recipes including that special Luigi pizza! John opened Meglio's on St. Charles Rock Road in 2005. Visit Meglio's Grill and Bar for excellent Italian food and flash back in time when you taste Luigi's pizza. www.megliositalian.com

Hendel's Restaurant

Everyone who lives in Florissant knows about Hendel's Restaurant, an incredibly good restaurant with a historic background. Hendel's opened in 1886 as a grocery store and did not become a restaurant until 1994. Currently owned by Nathan and Christina Bennet, they have an excellent menu and you will have the feel of Old Florissant with its French history. I first took my mother there for Mother's Day in 1995 and sat on the brick patio under the huge oak trees. We sipped pink lemonade that was spiced up a bit. She felt right at home, coming from a small town in Illinois. Take a trip to Hendel's, and experience the great food and the history. That and much more can be found at: www.hendelsrestaurant.com

Jacks or Better

Remember eating the peanuts, throwing the shells on the floor and having a great burger? Jacks or Better on West Florissant and on Lindbergh were two of many stops when we were cruizin' around North County. Before that, we may go by CMC Stereo to check out the latest 8 track car stereo and afterwards, we might head to Peaches for the newest records. These menu items should bring back a few good memories – hmmm good!

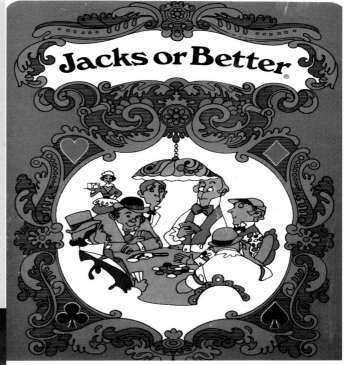

Lum's

Who remembers drag racing on Hall Street late at night in the '60s? One popular place to celebrate when you where done racing was Lum's at the corner of Hall Street and Riverview. There were other Lum's in St. Louis including St. Charles Rock Road, Lindbergh, and downtown by Famous Barr. My date then, now my wife, was a regular. I remember the tender roast beef sandwiches and the great burgers. Hope you remember Lum's and your special times there.

Faraci's

Faraci's, a long-time favorite in Ferguson and North County, was opened by Joe Faraci in 1968. They moved to their current location on Florissant Road in 1980. Dine in or carry-out, Faraci's has great pizza, pasta and salads — try the fantastic Faraci Special (sausage, pepperoni, bacon, mushrooms and onions). Stop by and see the owners Jim and Dawn Marshall and their daughter Amber. Pictured is the restaurant and Jim preparing Faraci's special sauce slow cooked in a huge pot. It's used for many dishes and made from scratch like everything on their menu.

Burcke's

When the streetcar line stopped running to Florissant in the 1930s, the Narrow Gauge Depot became Burcke's confectionary. William Burcke bought the building at the corner of St. Ferdinand and St. Catherine and added living quarters. In the 1950s he added a section to the building and car hops to wait on customers. Burcke's was the place to go for a burger, hot dog, malt or ice cream soda. Historic Florissant bought the building in the late 1960s, restored it, and moved to Tower Court Park. Pictured are the Burckes and their car hops. William Burcke Jr. is on the left and his father William Burcke is behind him.

Bergjan's Dairy

Bergjan's Dairy on S. Florissant Road opened in 1955 and was the place to go for a cone, malt, sundae, bakery goods and more. Today, Doozle's Custard continues the tradition. Paul Kohmen became familiar with the dairy business at an early age, delivering milk with his grandfather while riding with him on the way to Sacred Heart School. The milk products were supplied by Bergjan's Dairy on St. Charles Rock Road. Recognizing the desire for ice cream and dairy products, Paul opened his dairy store which soon became a popular place. Besides serving many families, the dairy also regularly entertained high school students from Aquinas and McCluer. Especially after football practice, the guys would show up and down a huge cup of milk with a few Hostess cupcakes. Soon, the kids would gather around his sign on the corner and wait for friends to cruize by. Paul eventually changed the name of his place to Kohnen's. The dairy closed in 1982. Stop by Doozles for great concretes, shakes, banana splits, slushes and more. Pictured is Paul in the dairy in 1955, the outside of Kohnen's and Doozle's. www.doozlesfrozencustard.com

Ole Topper

A Glasgow Village and North County landmark on Chambers Road. Opened in 1939, this was the place for a cold beer with the guys after work, cooling off, storytelling after 18 holes of golf or meeting with friends and listening to the jukebox. While 'not quite' of age, we also enjoyed a few cold beverages at the Topper. Pictured is a group of regulars including Tom Stankey, Jim Linahan, Jim Parteo, Jack Sheridan, Jeep Hayes, Harold Vogt, Mike Kelvel, Butch Chandler, Jerry Donovan, and John Donahau. The Ole Topper is now the Leprechaun Gold Bar. Stop by for another cold one!

Saullo's

Stan and Agnes Saullo came to America from Sicily and brought their recipes for excellent food with them. Before opening their current location at 11040 Larimore Road, they had restaurants on Goodfellow and West Florissant. Stan's grandson, Vito, runs Saullo's, with Stan still working his magic in the kitchen. Stop by Saullo's and see Vito for excellent pizza, salads, pasta and sandwhiches.

Helfer's Pastries & Deli Cafe

Chris and Kathy Helfer met as teens working at Marie's Bakery in Florissant. Little did they know a 'sweet' life was in front of them. They had bakeries in Arnold and Ballwin, but wanted to return to their roots in Florissant. In 1980 they opened Helfer's Pastries in an A-frame building next to Don McElroy's 7th Street Meat Market (the A-frame used to be a Das Wienerhaus!). In 1992 they moved next door to their current location, 380 St. Ferdinand Street. Helfer's Pastries & Deli Cafe is known for their quality. Customers come from all over the St. Louis area for Helfer's pastries and deli sandwiches made from scratch using many family recipes. Try their famous original St. Louis gooey butter cake and strawberry and whipped cream pastries.
www.helferspastries.com

Pine Lawn Steak 'n Shake

Cruizin'! The destination was Steak 'n Shake on Natural Bridge. You'd drive there with a car full of friends and have burgers, fries and cokes delivered to the car on the tray. Then, drive around in circles, park next to others, talk or change cars and then drive in circles. Eating is optional but driving in circles is required. No dining and dashing!

Rosciglione Bakery

In 1898, Vincenzo Rosciglione opened the first Italian bakery in "Little Italy" in downtown St. Louis. His son Peter and his wife Rose took over the bakery in 1949 and it moved to Dellwood. In 1997, Rosciglione moved to its present location on Bluestone in St. Charles. Fourth generation Francesco 'Peter' Rosciglione and his wife Pam continue the family tradition. Their selection includes over 40 types of delicious Italian cookies, stollens, pastries, Italian pudding, and Sicilian Cassatha cakes filled with ricotta. But, oh, those cannolis, they are the best! Rosciglione's also has a wide variety of Italian grocery items, gelati, lemon ice, homemade sandwiches and other ready-made items. Platters and wedding cakes can be custom made. Stop by for delicious Italian delicacies. Pictured is the Rosciglione's Bakery in Dellwood, celebrating Pete's birthday, and their current St. Charles location. www.rosciglionebakery.com

Fratelli's Ristorante

In 1948, newlyweds Tommaso and Francesca Alagna emigrated to the U.S. from Sicily. They did not have great wealth but shared a love for cooking. They collected special family recipes, perfected them in their American kitchen and, with their two sons Joe and Tom, opened Tommaso's Italian Restaurant on Airport Road in Ferguson in 1970. Tommaso's quickly became a St. Louis favorite. In 1983, Joe and Tom opened Fratelli's, a small restaurant in Dellwood. Now located in St. Charles at 2061 Zumbehl Road, the Fratelli brothers continue the family heritage of excellent Italian food and customer service. Visit Fratelli's and try their spaghetti, pollo piccata, eggplant parmigiano or spedini. Pictured are Fratelli's restaurant in Dellwood and their current St. Charles location.
www.fratellisristorante.com

Roberto's Italian Restaurant

Robert and Margaret (Bob and Peggy) Camenzind opened Roberto's in 1962 very near the restaurant's current location. It had only a couple booths and tables. They worked long hours; because they both had day jobs, they ran the restaurant at night and stayed open late for the neighborhood shift workers. Their hard work paid off as they expanded to the current location, growing to 17 tables and a bigger carryout business. In 2000, after 38 years running the restaurant, Bob and Peggy retired. Janice, their daughter, took over the business and expanded again in 2006. She continued the family tradition with her parents' very same recipes. Able to accommodate larger groups while serving regular customers, Roberto's takes pride in their 49-year tradition of excellent food and customer service. Visit Roberto's at #16 Mullanphy Garden Shopping Center (Mullanphy and Shackelford) for great pizza, salads and a variety of Italian dishes. Pictured are the original dining room and Roberto's today. www.robertositalianstl.com

III. "HOME COOKIN'"

Tasty Recipes

Hendel's Tomato Basil Cream Sauce

2 oz. butter

1/4 tbsp minced garlic

1/2 cup diced tomato

1 tbsp basil flakes

4 oz. white wine

1/2 tsp chicken base

3 cups 40% cream

Salt and w. pepper

Make roux to thicken (coat a spoon)

Add 1 tomato (seeded and julienned)

Add 6 fresh basil leaves (julienned)

Grone's Cafeteria Pineapple Upsidedown Cake

Caramel Smear – combine and cream together: 1/4 lb. butter, 1/2 lb. brown sugar, 2 tbsp white kero syrup. Once creamed, spread evenly in bottom of 9" x 13" pan. Place 12 slices of canned pineapple and arrange evenly on top of smear. Place maraschino cherry half in hole of pineapple slice. Spread chopped pecans on top of smear that is not covered with pineapple. Prepare a yellow cake mix (Duncan Hines) and pour on top of pineapple and pecans. Bake at 350º for approximately 45 minutes. When done flip pan upside down and remove pan ASAP. Cool and serve.

Rizzo's Florissant Sole Cardinale

4 ounces of filet of sole breaded &

deep fried in Italian bread crumbs

2 cups water

1/2 cup Chablis white wine

1/4 cup lemon juice

3/4 cup frozen peas

1 cup thinly sliced button mushrooms

1-1/2 cups grated provel

1/2 stick butter

1/2 cup of flour

1 tsp chicken base

Bring the water, wine and lemon juice to a boil. Make a roux with 1/2 stick of butter and 1/2 cup of flour. Add water, wine and lemon juice. Add 1 teaspoon of chicken base and thicken sauce with shredded provel cheese. Add peas and mushrooms. Cover sole with sauce, garrish with lemon slices, and enjoy. Serves 4.

Cristo's Restaurant
Thousand Island Salad Dressing

3 hard boiled eggs chipped large

1/4 oz ground black pepper

1/4 oz salt

8 oz can chili sauce

6 oz can diced pimentos

3 oz pickle relish

1 qt salad dressing

Mix well and chill.

Cristo's Restaurant Meatloaf

2 lbs. ground beef
Grind 1/4 onion & 1/8 stalk celery
Sautee onion and celery, add to beef.
1 egg
4 oz bottle catsup
1/2 tsp steak seasoning
1/2 cup bread crumbs
3/4 oz Worcestershire L&P
Mix all ingredients well, mold into loaf.
Bake at 350° to 140°.

Lombardo's Italian Sausage A La Lombardo

2 tbsp margarine or butter
2 oz green bell pepper, sliced julienne
2 oz onion, sliced julienne
2 whole tomatoes, peeled, sliced julienne
1/4 cup sherry wine
1/4 cup beef or veal stock
Cooked linguine or pasta choice
Italian sausage links, broiled or grilled
Chopped fresh parsley

In skillet, melt margarine. Cook green bell peppers, onion, and tomatoes, stirring often, until al dente. Drain. Add wine, then stock. Continue to cook until heated thoroughly. Add cooked pasta of choice. To serve, place pasta mixture in bowl. Top with sausage. Sprinkle with parsley. Serves 1

Yacovelli's Parmesan-Encrusted Tilapia

1 cup Italian bread crumbs
1 cup Parmesan cheese
Four 7 oz tilapia filets
1/2 white onion, chopped
1/2 tomato, fresh, chopped
1/4 cup olive oil
1 tsp leaf oregano
1 tsp basil

Breading mixture: Mix bread crumbs and Parmesan cheese together.
Wet tilapia in water and dredge in breading mixture. Place in small baking dish and add water to cover bottom of dish. Bake uncovered for approximately 7 minutes at 450°. While fish is cooking, sauté onions and tomatoes in olive oil until onions are lightly browned, approximately 3-4 minutes. Add spices and simmer on low heat until fish is done. Pour over tilapia and serve. Serves 4.

Top of the Tower Spinning Salad

1 (3 oz) package cream cheese, softened
3 oz blue cheese, crumbled
5 to 6 tbsp water
1-1/2 tsp Worcestershire sauce
6 cups torn iceberg lettuce leaves
1/4 cup red wine vinegar
1/4 tsp prepared mustard or to taste
1 cup endive leaves or to taste
1 hard-cooked egg, chopped
Seasoned salt
Freshly ground black pepper
8 anchovy filets

2 tbsp snipped chives
2 tbsp salad-sandwich sauce (such as Durkee)
1 raw egg (see note)
4-1/2 tsp lemon juice
1 cup vegetable oil, divided or to taste
3-1/2 cups torn romaine lettuce
3/4 tsp paprika
3/4 tsp salt
1/4 tsp garlic powder
1/2 tsp ground white pepper
1 tbsp granulated sugar

Combine cream cheese and blue cheese; beat until smooth.
Gradually beat in water until mixture is of pouring consistency. Set aside.
Place raw egg, lemon juice and 1/4 cup oil in blender. Blend on medium speed for 15 seconds.
Increase speed; slowly add remaining 3/4 cup oil.
Add vinegar, mustard, paprika, salt, garlic powder, white pepper, sugar, chives, salad-sandwich sauce and
Worcestershire sauce. Blend until smooth.
In salad bowl, mix iceberg, romaine and endive.
Pour in enough of each dressing to coat greens.
Sprinkle with chopped egg and seasoned salt and black pepper to taste.
Toss gently three times. Garnish with anchovies.

Note: To avoid the small risk of salmonella, use a pasteurized whole egg or 1/2 cup egg substitute. Serves 4 to 6.

Meglios' Italian Grill and Bar Luxurious Scalloped Potatoes

3 tbsp butter

3 tbsp all purpose flour

1/4 tsp pepper

6 medium potatoes peeled and sliced thin

1 small onion, finely chopped

1 tsp salt

2 1/4 cups heavy cream

1 tbsp butter

Heat oven to 350°. Grease bottom and sides of a 2-quart casserole with shortening. Melt 3 tbsp of butter in 2-quart sauce pan over medium heat. Cook onion in butter about 2 minutes, stirring occasionally, until tender.

Stir in flour, salt, and pepper. Cook, stirring constantly, until smooth and bubbly; remove from heat.

Stir in heavy cream. Heat to boiling, stirring constantly. Boil and stir for 1 minute.

Layer potatoes in casserole. Pour sauce over potatoes. Cut 1 tbsp of butter into small pieces; sprinkle over potatoes.

Cover and bake for 30 minutes. Uncover and bake about 1 hour or until potatoes are tender.

Let stand 5 to 10 minutes before serving. The sauce thickens as it stands.

Slice into squares and serve as an accompaniment to your entrée. Serves 9 to 12.

Rosciglione's Honey Clusters (Strufoli)

2 cups sifted flour

1/4 tsp salt

1 cup honey

3 eggs

1/4 tsp vanilla

1 tbsp sugar

Combine dry ingredients. Add one egg at a time and vanilla until dough is soft.

Turn dough onto a lightly floured surface and knead. Divide dough into halves.

Lightly roll the first half 1/4 inch thick to form a rectangle. Cut dough with pastry cutter into strips 1/4 inch wide.

Use palm of hand to roll strips to pencil thickness. Cut into pieces about 1/4 to 1/2 inch long.

Deep fry 365° 3 to 5 minutes. Drain on absorbent paper.

Cook in skillet over low heat for about 5 minutes: 1 cup honey, 1 tbsp of sugar. Add deep-fried pieces and coat.

Refrigerate to chill slightly. Remove to a large serving platter and arrange in a cone-shaped mound.

Sprinkle with 1 tbsp of tiny multicolored nonpareils. Serves 8 to 10.

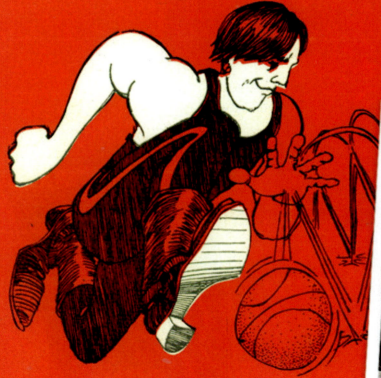

NORMANDY'S FORTY-THIRD CHRISTMAS

INVITATIONAL BASKETBALL TOURNAMENT

DECEMBER 26, 27, 29, 30, 31, 1975

Valley Of The Flowers

Glen Echo

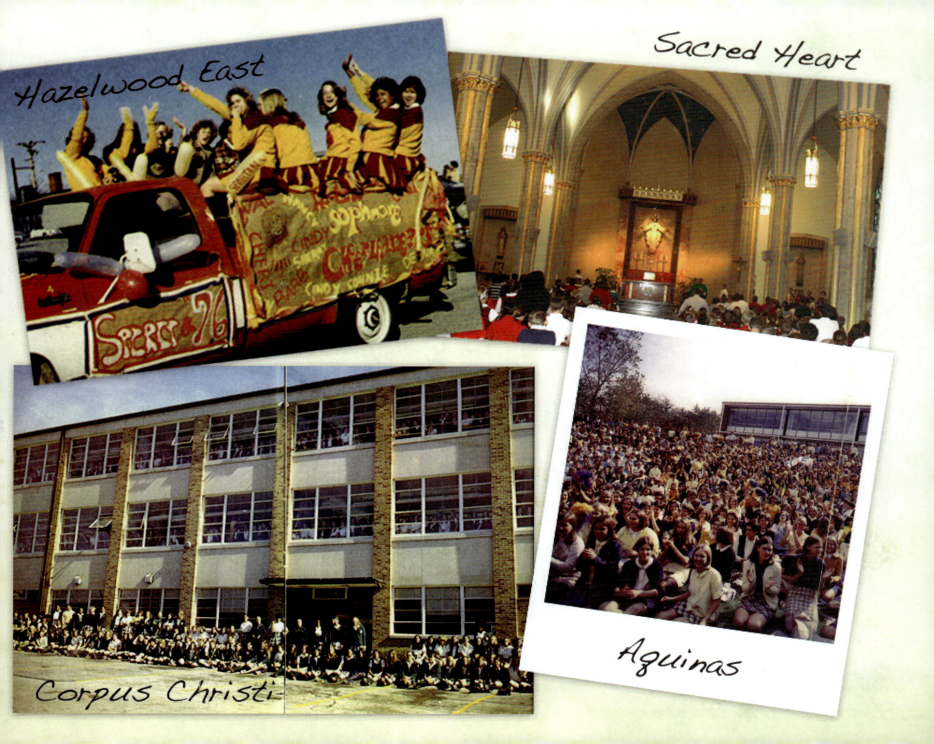

RIVERVIEW

Pattonville

Rosary

BIG FOOT

LaRocca's Chicken Parmesan

4 skinless, boneless, chicken breast (about 1 1/2 - 2 lbs)

1/4 cup Virgin Olive Oil

1/2 cup flour

2 large eggs

2 tbsp milk

1 cup bread crumbs, Italian blend

Salt & Pepper

1 ball fresh Buffalo Mozzarella, about 8 oz, water drained and sliced thin

Fresh grated Parmesan

Homemade or your favorite marinara sauce

Preheat the oven to 400 degrees. Place the chicken breast between two pieces of
plastic wrap and pound them with a flat meat mallet, until they are about a 1/2 inch thick.

Put the flour in a shallow pan and season with salt and pepper.

In a bowl whip together the eggs and milk until well blended.

Put the bread crumbs in a shallow pan or platter.

Set your ingredients up in this order so you have a small assembly line.

In a large non-stick skillet on medium heat add the olive oil. When the oil is hot you are ready for the chicken.

Lightly dredge the chicken cutlets in the flour, and then dip them in the egg wash completely coating them.

Let the excess drip off, and then dredge in the breadcrumbs.

Add the breaded chicken to the skillet and fry for about 4-5 minutes on each side or until crispy and golden brown,
turning only once. Remove from heat.

Place the chicken into a baking dish, ladle the marinara sauce over the chicken, sprinkle with parmesan and top with the
mozzarella slices. Bake for 15 minutes or until the cheese is bubbly. Serves 4.

Russo's Catering Italian Sesame Cookies (Biscotti di Giugiulena)

1/2 lb. butter

1 cup sugar

3 eggs

6 – 8 drops anise oil

3 cups flour

2-1/2 tsp baking powder

1 cup sesame seeds

Preheat oven to 375°. Grease two cookie sheets. In a large bowl cream together butter and sugar; add eggs and anise oil; mix thoroughly. Sift together flour and baking powder; mix together with egg and sugar mixture. Form pieces of dough into oblong cookies resembling 2-inch long breadsticks. Roll cookies in sesame seeds and place on greased cookie sheets.
Bake for 10-12 minutes until lightly browned. Baking time: 1 hour; makes 3 dozen.

Helfer's Bakery and Deli - Dad's Potato Salad, aka Grandpa B's Potato Salad

4 cups sliced cooked potatoes

1/4 cup clear French dressing

3 hard cooked eggs, diced

1 cup celery, sliced

3 tbsp onion, diced

1/3 cup sweet pickle relish

1/2 cup mayonnaise or salad dressing

Potatoes have better flavor if cooked with skins on. Cut up potatoes while warm. Marinate cut-up potatoes in French dressing 1 hour. Add remaining ingredients, season to taste with salt and pepper. Herb seasoning salt substitute may be used instead of salt and pepper. Garnish with sliced hard-boiled egg, parsley and pimento. Sprinkle with paprika if desired.

Fratelli's Penne Ala Salute

1 28 oz. can peeled Italian-style pear tomatoes
3 cloves garlic
1 teaspoon salt
1/2 teaspoon black pepper
1/3 cup extra virgin olive oil
1/4 cup fresh basil
2 cups broccoli florets
1/2 cup sliced sun-dried tomatoes
1 cup sliced mushrooms
1/4 cup grated Asiago cheese or Romano cheese
4 cups cooked penne pasta cooked al dente (1/2 lb. uncooked pasta)

Sauce: In a food processor, mince garlic, olive oil and salt & pepper together for one minute.
Cut Italian-style tomatoes into small pieces (about 1" cubes), reserve some liquid.
In a bowl combine garlic & olive oil mixture with cut tomatoes, add chopped fresh basil. Set aside.
Place pasta, broccoli, mushrooms and sun-dried tomatoes in a one-gallon pot of rapidly boiling salt water.
When water boils again, drain.
Toss pasta together with sauce mixture in a large bowl. Serve immediately.
Sprinkle pasta with grated Asiago cheese, fresh basil and drizzle with extra virgin olive oil. Makes 4 servings.

IV. Big Screen

Popular Drive-Ins and Theaters

Savoy Theater

Located in the heart of downtown Ferguson, the Savoy opened in 1936 with 632 seats. It became a Wehrenberg theater in 1966 and closed in 1993. It was the neighborhood theater for Saturday afternoon matinees and as teenagers, those date night movies. In the early days, 25 cents would buy a ticket and popcorn! A real plus – the Savoy even had its own sweet and cigarette store right next door.

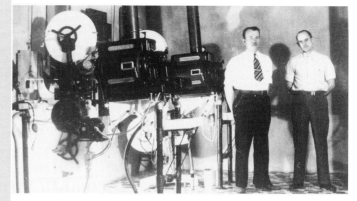

Olympic Drive-In

One of the more popular pictures in Cruizin' North County, we had to include another picture of the 'Big O' with those famous black curtains on the Rock Road looking a bit 'tattered'!

JANET THEATER

Who in Jennings can forget the Janet Theater on West Florissant? The Janet was built in the 1930s. It was a great place for a date or for a family movie, then to Steak 'n Shake for a burger or to Bart's Malt Shop. If we were really good, Mom and Dad would take us to Zimmerman's. Pictured are the kids in the area who flocked to the Janet for a movie with friends in the cool air conditioning.

270 DRIVE-IN

When this new drive-in opened in 1964, it was THE place to go with a big screen, good speakers and even heaters for your car. The concession stand was huge and it carried a big selection of good food. The 270 could accommodate 1,200 cars and was the largest in the area at that time. The yellow tower and blinking red ball could be seen for miles. It was demolished in 1981 but the memories, whether in the front seat, back seat or sitting on the hood or tailgate, live on.

Airway Drive-In

Growing up in Bellefontaine Neighbors, I was used to the North Drive-In or the T Bird near Goodfellow and Natural Bridge. But the Airway really impressed me when I made my first visit in my late teens. It was like something on the Vegas strip with the lights, huge entrance and the bigger-than-life neon majorette twirling the baton, complemented by the light towers. Driving though those gates was a totally different experience, making me feel I was far from home – like a vacation! The Airway opened in 1950 and could hold 1,000 cars. Sadly, it was torn down in 1986, but the majorette and towers live on as do the memories of going with friends, partying, hanging out and maybe even watching a movie.

Spanish Lake Cinema

Originally opened as the Jerry Lewis Cinema in 1972, it later became the Spanish Lake Cinema then the Belle Park Cinema. The Linda Lovelace 'family' movie created quite a stir and led to the closure of the Spanish Lake Cinema. For at least part of its history, it was a popular neighborhood theater and a great place to go with friends.

Wellston Theatre

The original Wellston Theatre opened in 1922 at 6226 Easton Avenue, which today is Dr. Martin Luther King Drive. It was destroyed by a fire in 1944, and the new Wellston opened in November 1945. It held 950 people and packed them in for every show. It was a beautiful theatre with a terrazzo floor on the outside walkway that led into the lobby, a huge concession stand in the middle of the lobby, and a grand staircase on each side of the lobby. Memories include watching countless matinees for a dime and sitting through movies over and over. Many of the guys who went to Wellston High worked at the Wellston, resplendent in their uniforms.

V. PAPA'S GOT A BRAND NEW BAG

Favorite Stores and Malls

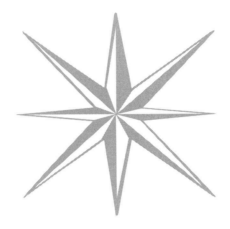

Robert Hall

On Riverview Drive next to Dairy Queen, a popular place for men's clothes at a discount, including suits, shirts, ties and more. In the mid-'50s you could purchase a suit for $32!

Black Jack

Black Jack: where Old Halls Ferry intersects with Parker Road. Stores and shops over the years include Black Jack Hardware Store, Angelo's Pizza, Sexauer's Market, the Moose Lodge, Benny's Tavern and Valenti's Market. Did you know Black Jack got its name from a grove of large Black Jack oak trees that stood at that intersection? In the 1800s it was a popular place for farmers to rest as they took their crops to markets closer to the city.

Village Square

Opened in the mid-'60s, there was so much to do at Village Square in Hazelwood. Stores and entertainment venues included Golde's, Dot Drugs, Kresge's, Flaming Pit, Village Inn and the Village Square Theater. It opened with one screen, but by 1985 there were six. Village Square was frequented by many high school students from Aquinas, McCluer, Hazelwood and others.

Ferguson

Downtown Ferguson was, and is, a popular destination for North County residents and others from across the area. Pictured is a view of downtown Ferguson in the 1950s, which included stores such as King Drugs, Mannino's, Olie's Barber Shop, Velvet Freeze, Ferguson Department Store, Montrey's, Graf Motor Company, and Day and Night Market.

Ferguson Department Store

It was 'the' place to shop in downtown Ferguson, whether it was back-to-school clothes, a new dress, shoes or a suit. It was opened in 1935 by Steve Weber. For years it housed the Missouri License Office in the back of the store. All of the best-dressed residents shopped at the Ferguson Department Store. Pictured is a Ferguson Department Store window with women's fashions. The Northern Arts Council (NAC) occupied the Ferguson Department Store until recently. NAC is a nonprofit organization that supports and promotes the arts and culture in North St. Louis County. Comprised of volunteers, NAC hosts public exhibits and offers hands-on opportunities at community and local special events. They sponsor guest artists at the Ferguson Farmer's Market and hold public exhibits at CORK Wine Bar and Ferguson Brewing Company in downtown Ferguson.
www.facebook.com/NorthernArtsCouncil.com

GLASGOW VILLAGE SHOPPING CENTER

In the heart of Glasgow Village, its stores and restaurants included Cusumano's, Ben Franklin, Tom Boy, Tony's, Bonnie Bell's, and Rinderer's Rexall Drug Store. Neighbors walked to the shopping center to do their shopping or enjoy a meal, and the kids rode their bikes. I remember a late night trip to Rinderer's, as it was the only place in North County who carried the right 'binky' for one of our children.

NORMANDY SHOPPING CENTER

At the corner of Natural Bridge and Lucas and Hunt, it had a variety of places to eat, shop, and have fun. Britt's, Normandy Bowl, Holland House, Western Auto, Walgreens, Velvet Freeze, Harpers, Ben Franklin, National, Doy TV, Shoe Rack and more. My brother-in-law bought his 'threads' at Britts and remembers sporting some cool blue-and-white checked pants in the '60s!

Fischer's

With roots in Florissant dating back to 1934 on Jefferson, this family-owned business remains a popular North County store. Initially selling and repairing shoes and harnesses, Fischer's expanded to dry goods in the late 1930s. Henry Fischer turned the business over to his sons Al and Jim. In 1954 the store was moved to its current location and expanded in 1958 (pictured are Al, Henry and Jim). The expansion included sporting goods, which is Fisher's focus today. I remember taking my children to Fisher's for school uniforms, ball gloves and all types of sports equipment. Visit Jack Fisher and his team at Fisher's for a wide selection of sporting goods at reasonable prices. You'll be treated like one of the family!
www.fischerssports.com

Paul's Market

Opened in 1960, Paul's is a long-time Ferguson mainstay on Elizabeth Avenue. Paul Crump and his friendly staff welcome shoppers with excellent meats, groceries, and years ago, oh that penny candy! Children and teenagers would choose their favorite penny candy from the big selection or buy a soda or ice cream. Gary Crump, his wife Tracy and his son Alex continue the tradition with not only groceries but fresh meats and barbequed pork, beef and ribs made in their smoker with a tasty BBQ sauce. Stop by for a great meal to go with all the fixings or for something to cook, all at reasonable prices. Gary's staff makes you feel right at home, and he believes in giving back to the community by partnering with several charities, including the Variety Club. Paul's Market, "the biggest little steak store in St. Louis," exemplifies the spirit and neighborhood feeling of Ferguson from days when life was a bit simpler. Pictured are the original Paul's Market, a visit from the "Wienermobile," and Paul's today.

Ben Franklin/Nagle's

Remember the Ben Franklin in Glasgow Village Shopping Center? It was a great 5 & 10 store. Owner Joe Nagle would greet you, as would their pet bird Benny – he was a talker! The penny candy selection was huge and included Bit 'O Honey, Dots, Double Bubble, Sweet Tarts, Bazooka, Lik-a-Maid, and on and on. Kids stopped by several times a week after school with their dimes to buy bags of penny candy. On Saturday mornings, they would get Beatle trading cards and baseball cards with the great gum. Joe's son Mike, pictured in front of the store, grew up in the business.

In 1968, Joe opened a second store in the Mullanphy Gardens Shopping Center. Mike and Jeannie opened Nagle's on Patterson Road in 1986 and are celebrating their 25th anniversary this year. If you can't find it at Nagle's, it probably doesn't exist. Gifts, house wares, school and party supplies, toys and more, not to mention a Nagle tradition, the massive penny candy selection! Visit Nagle's, meet Mike and Jeannie and experience a true North County tradition. (Even Santa, who appears the first week in December every year at Nagle's, likes Cruizin' North County!)

Valenti's

In 1937, Frank Valenti's grandfather opened Valenti's at Jefferson and Cass. Frank's father and uncle took over the business and ran a store on Vandeventer and Maffit. After losing his father and uncle in a hold up and shooting, young Frank took over the business until 1980 when they moved to Black Jack on Parker and Halls Ferry. After working for another market for a short time, Frank opened Valenti's on Mexico Road in St. Peters. Valenti's Meat Market and Bakery offers a variety of freshly prepared sandwiches and meals such as spedini, lasagna and veal parmesan. They have an excellent selection of meats that can be custom cut as well as pies and bread that are made fresh every day. Valenti's also offers several catering services including weddings, meetings, special events and deli express.
www.valentismarket.com

7th Street Meat Market

Excellent meats including Italian specialities, deli sandwiches, freshly baked bread and pastries, and Italian gifts. Well known for their tasty sausita and spedini meat – they were the best! The market was founded in 1912 by Alfred Accardi on 7th Street in downtown St. Louis. It moved to Dellwood and eventually was sold to Don McElroy. The market and adjoining buildings on St. Ferdinand were built in 1979. There are many fond memories of shopping at 7th Street and enjoying family meals using their products. Pictured are the market and Don's familiar 1926 Model 'T'.

Day and Night Market/Mannino's

A family-owned Italian store dating back to the 1930s. Mannino's Day and Night Market, which later became Mannino's Market, was a popular store in Ferguson. Founded by Phillip and Josephine Mannino, fourth-generation Tony Mannino runs the Cottleville store and continues to hand-select the produce for that store and the one in Flint Hill. Visit Mannino's, see their butchers and enjoy their produce and freshly baked pies and bread.
www.manninosmarket.com

VI. IT'S ALL IN THE GAME
Games We Played

GLEN ECHO COUNTRY CLUB

Opened on May 25, 1901 as the first club designed for 18 holes west of the Mississippi. Glen Echo hosted the 1904 Olympic golf matches and is the oldest Olympic venue in continuous daily use in the world. It is also the only venue of its type allowed to fly the Olympic flag. Known primarily as a golf club, Glen Echo is moving toward becoming more family friendly with clay tennis courts and a new aquatic park. Fine and casual dining as well as banquet and private rooms are available in the beautiful clubhouse. Pictured is the original Glen Echo Clubhouse, members arriving by stagecoach on opening day 1901 – check out their attire and the golf bags – and an aerial view of the club from the 1920's. Note St. Ann's Parish behind the clubhouse, the St. Vincent Home for Children on the right and North County in the distance. www.gecc.org

Norwood Hills Country Club

Featured in Cruizin' North County, Norwood offers a variety of activities for the entire family. Pictures from the 1960s include an aerial view of the Clubhouse, the annual Easter Buffet and Egg Hunt (a club tradition), and the old bar in the clubhouse. Also pictured are a group of Norwood Hills caddies getting instructions for the day. In those days, a caddie could make $2.00 to $2.50 per round.
www.norwoodhills.com

Normandie Golf Club

Opened in October 1901, Normandie was considered a 'players' club and was very popular with the Cardinals. Dizzy Dean was among those who played there. The legendary Babe Ruth also played the course. Normandie was a private club until 1985 when it was opened to the public. Normandie, like Glen Echo, the original Bellerive and other Foulis brothers-designed courses, attempted to recreate the shot values they recalled from their days playing the links of St. Andrews. It remains one of the most challenging public layouts in the area. Pictured is the club house in the 1970s.
www.normandiegolf.com

Normandy Basketball Tournament

Dating back to the late 1930s, when only four teams played (Ritenour, Normandy, Wellston and Ferguson), the Normandy High School Basketball Tournament is held the last week in December. For decades it was THE high school tournament in the area, growing to 32 teams in two divisions: green and red. You could arrive at 9:00 am and watch 13 straight hours of basketball. A new gym built in 1970 replaced the 'pit' style field house that was built in the 1930s. When a team was playing, their light or a huge board blinked, but when they lost, their light went out. This rich tradition of the Normandy Tournament continues today. Pictured is a 1950 game between Normandy and McBride, as well as the tournament program covers from 1973 and 1975.

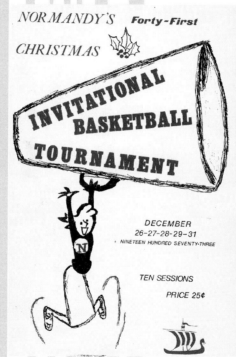

St. Vincent's Home for Children Basketball Tournament

A popular North County grade school basketball tournament dating back to the 1950s. St. Vincent's was founded in 1850, and the current home in Normandy was built in 1917. St. Vincent's endured the Civil War, the Great Depression, two World Wars and numerous other conflicts, all of which brought orphans to the home. Today, St. Vincent's continues to serve youth in need as a residential treatment center. Pictured are a 1962 game between Ascension Grade School (white) and Little Flower (dark). Note the team banners of St. Lucy, St. Kevin, and Sts. John and James, as well as students and parents cheering for their teams. www.saintvincenthome.org

Dick Weber Lanes

Dick Weber and bowling are synonymous. Along with Bob Timme, Dick owned Dick Weber Lanes on Washington Street. What a great place to go with the guys or a date, or you may have been in one of many leagues. Dick's awards and recognitions are too numerous to mention, but he is a member of the US Bowling Congress Hall of Fame, the PBA Hall of Fame and the St. Louis Walk of Fame. He was also a founding member of the Professional Bowlers Association. A big believer in teaching youth the game of bowling, Dick Weber hosted the finals of the Youth Games in 1968. Dick was also a frequent visitor on The Late Show with David Letterman, rolling balls on a lane outside the studio into bizarre items. A tireless ambassador for the game of bowling, Dick passed away in 2005. Florissant, North County and St. Louis were fortunate to have Dick Weber and are thankful for all of his contributions. Pictured are some participants in the Youth Bowling Games with Dick and Ed McCauly and the current ABF Dick Weber Lanes marquee – stop by and have some fun!

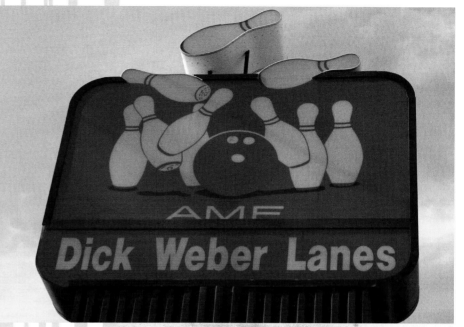

Ferguson Bowl

In 1939, Bill Niehaus opened Ferguson Bowling Lanes, the first commercial bowling alley in North County. It started with eight lanes and had numerous church- and organization-sponsored teams. Automatic pinsetters were installed in 1956 and eight more lanes were added. In 1957, Dick Weber, of the Budweiser Team, and Ken Wasser bowled at the grand re-opening. Many students from Ferguson and Florissant grade and high schools, as well as UMSL, learned to bowl at Ferguson Lanes. Ken Wasser became the owner of the lanes in 1950 and later it was passed to his sons. Ferguson Lanes closed in 1968. Pictured are the original lanes and the 10-Pin Inn Restaurant in the front of the building. Many memories of fun times at Ferguson Bowl.

CREST BOWL

Some things never change, including fun times at Crest Bowl, a favorite in Florissant for years. Since 1958, Crest Bowl is the place you bowl with friends, in a league, or to celebrate a birthday – cosmically of course! Do you remember when Crest had 24 lanes and a miniature golf course? Enjoy Soup's Sports Bar and Grill, join a Youth League, or show your talents with Mr. Karaoke. Come over to Crest, and Greg Campbell and Mike Flanagan will take care of you. Pictured are the ground breaking of Crest, the way it used to look, and bowlers today having fun in one of many leagues.

Other North County bowling lanes: Red Crown, Airport Bowl, Lucky Strike, North County Lanes, Bowl-Ero, Maple, River Roads, Northland, Silver Shield, Arcade, Tower, and Dellwood.

VII. "I Get Around"

Cruizin' Kids

Growing up in North County

Before we could cruize Circle Steak, we cruized on our bikes. We'd ride everywhere – to the park to play Indian ball, to school, to the confectionary (or Nagles!) to get penny candy, an RC Cola and some chips, to our Cub Scout meetings, or to the store to get bread and milk for Mom (they fit nicely in the basket on the front of our handle bars). If we had some extra change, we would get flip cards, hoping for a good Cardinal player, and that great tasting gum. The flip cards would end up on the back wheel of our bike hooked on with a clothes pin. What a cool sound! Pictured are the Holy Cross in Baden first graders visiting the Baden firehouse (note Jeannie Nagle in the 'fashionable' scarf of the day – pretty cute!); a Ferguson policeman directing Griffith school students with their bikes across Chambers Road; a Ferguson policeman keeping a watchful eye on trick-or-treaters; a bunch of Jennings guys hamming it up for the camera (remember the rolled up jeans?), and look at the price of gas – 20.9 cents! Finally, children as well as adults enjoying the Florissant Valley of the Flowers Parade in 1976 and getting a chance to meet Kit Bond.

VIII. "Fun, Fun, Fun"

Fun Places

More memories from two popular amusement parks in North County (both featured in Cruizin' North County), Chain of Rocks, and Holiday Hill

Chain of Rocks

Sky Garden Restaurant, the haunted house, the merry-go-round, an aerial view of the park, and two ladies ready for some fun.

100

Holiday Hill

Holiday Hill rides and bowling machines in the arcade.

Westlake

It might have seemed like a smaller version of the Highlands, but we had a blast at Westlake Park anyway. Who can forget the Tumble Bug, Circle Swings with Biplanes, fun house, pool or the roller coaster called the Thunderbolt, a cause of many headaches from the 1920s through the '50s. Westlake was located near the junction of Natural Bridge and the Old Rock Road. There were several fires over the years, and the last one on May 5, 1955 closed it for good. Many of the rides were connected, which made it harder to contain the fires. No matter, I'll never forget the memories, especially the first time my Dad took me to Westlake; it was something very special I'd never seen before.

Kiddie Land

Those who grew up in the '50s have to remember Kiddie Land on Page. The anticipation we had of driving out to Kiddie Land gave our parents fits. It was a mecca of small rides: the Ferris wheel, Tilt-a-Whirl, roller coaster, and more. There was also a fantastic dodgem ride. It was the first ride we ran to where we just waited to collide with everyone and do some damage. We hated to leave when it was time to head home but looked forward to our next visit.

BIGFOOT

How cool would it be to cruize through Steak 'n Shake in BIGFOOT! Whenever we drove down Lindbergh or 270, we had to look over at BIGFOOT parked in front of its home. Bob Chandler, his wife Marilyn, and Jim Kramer started it all by opening the Midwest Four Wheel Drive and Performance Center in 1975. Bob was a construction contractor who drove a 4x4 truck and found it did not stand up to his off-roading escapades. In 1981, Bob successfully drove BIGFOOT #1 over some junk cars in the fields of Thies's Farm at Hanley and Highway 70, and then did it again soon after at a stadium stunt. The rest is history.

Did you know?

- There have been 16 BIGFOOTS.
- BIGFOOT has racked up 25 championships and made numerous international appearances.
- The tires started at 48", then were 66" and are now 10'!
- BIGFOOT holds four Guinness records for long jumps, speed and height.
- Movie appearances include Take This Job and Shove It, Road House and more.

Visit the BIGFOOT web site: www.BIGFOOT4X4.com for more information and souvenirs.

BIGFOOT services all types of pick-up trucks at their location in Hazelwood.

Hodges Skating Rink

It was a special treat to go to Hodges Roller Rink in the late 1950s. My dad took me and some neighborhood friends from Florissant to skate there a few times. I remember the music we skated to sounded like carousel music and may have been played by an organist at the rink. Of course, we had to have a snack halfway through skating. My favorite was a big juicy dill pickle for a nickel wrapped in a waxed paper bag from the big pickle jar on the counter. Pictured is Hodges from the 1950s and a clown and young boys in front of a traveling roller rink.

Aloha Skating Rink

The place to meet your friends and make new ones in Florissant. Did you learn to roller skate at Aloha or teach your girlfriend how to skate? Remember the couples skate and those palm trees? So many good times at Aloha! Pictures are Mayor Tom Eagan and family enjoying an evening at the rink. There was also an Aloha rink in Spanish Lake.

Other Rinks
Remember Coachlite, Skate Palace and All Saints?

Farmers Club

On Halls Ferry close to Chambers, Farmer's Club, or Farmer's Grove, was the place for picnics, dances and family gatherings. When we were young, my grandparents belonged to a German organization who held a picnic at Farmer's Grove every summer. There were games, tons of food, and cold Garger's soda in a big trough filled with ice chunks – grape, cream, orange flavors and more. It was the best. 'Louie' the accordion player belted out the German polkas. In the evening, our parents would dance inside the club and enjoy a few more cold beers. As with many of you, we have many great memories of Farmer's Grove.

Dirty Nellie's

Located in the Red Barn on Dunn Road, Dirty Nellie's was a gathering place for the North County younger set. Known for their bands, booze, women's nights and wet t-shirt contests, it was the place to go. Unfortunately, Florissant's finest did not appreciate the wet t-shirt contests, but the memories and good times at Dirty Nellie's live on!

Badenfest

One of the benefits of growing up in North County was being able to take a short ride and join in the annual street party in Baden, the Badenfest. There were throngs of people, German bands, dancing, and booth after booth of food and games. And you had to down some cold beer in those famous buckets. It was the day of the year when people from across St. Louis came to Baden to celebrate the success of a great neighborhood and its German heritage. Can't you still smell the bratwurst on the pit? So many memories! Willkommen to Baden!

January Walbash Park

Ferguson's 'jewel,' the park that has something for everyone. Since 1948, Ferguson's residents and others from across the area have enjoyed fishing at the well-stocked spring-fed lake, swimming in the pool on a hot summer's day, listening to a concert at the bandshell or picnicking with the family. Pictured are the bandshell, pool, lake with skaters, the January Walbash Building, and a scene from the snack shop.

Florissant Valley of the Flowers Festival

A celebration held in early May to welcome spring. Started in the early '60s, 2012 will be its 50th anniversary. The festival is held at several venues including the James J. Eagan Center, Koch Park, Old Town Florissant, Saint Ferdinand Shrine and the Duchesne Knights of Columbus Grounds. Pictured are Mayor Eagan crowning the 1973 Valley of the Flowers Queen, Diane Lemke, and the 1976 Queen and her court.

CASTAWAY CLUB

The Castaway Club was a teen nightclub in Ferguson located under a grocery store on Airport Road. It was the place to go for North County teens to have fun, dance, be with friends and hear some great bands. Dan Duncan, an MC and regular at the Club, recalls a band called the Sheratons and one of their members, Mike McDonald, of Doobie Brothers fame. Other popular bands included Acid Sette, the Good Feelin', the Aardvarks, and national bands like Blood Sweat and Tears, Chuck Berry, Bob Kuban, and Albert King. His favorite memory is when Kenny Rogers and the First Edition played the Club and borrowed a friend's bass amp and promptly blew out the speakers. There was also a group called Hourglass, an early incarnation of the Allman Brothers. He remembers the Allman Brothers' trademark blond hair swaying back and forth as they played their hearts out. Pictured are Acid Sette (which later became The Truth) and their fans, and their members on the wall between the snack bar and the dance floor. Also, Bob Kuban performing and Ray and DeDe Schulte with the wall-of-fame in the background.

The Admiral

Thanks for the Memories!

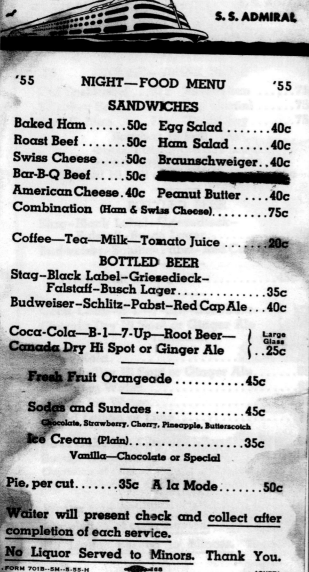

IX. "PLEASANT VALLEY SUNDAY"

Churches

Pleasant Valley Sunday

North County has a rich history of churches from a variety of religions. Two of historical note are Sacred Heart and Old St. Ferdinand Shrine.

Sacred Heart Catholic Church

In 1866 the Archbishop of St. Louis granted the request of German families in Florissant to establish a new parish, Church of the Sacred Heart of Jesus. The church was rebuilt in 1893, except for the steeple, which remains today. The convent building still stands at the corner of St. Louis and Jefferson Street. A new school was opened in 1952. Sacred Heart Parish remains a vibrant part of Florissant. The parishioners welcome you to join the Sacred Heart Family. Pictured are the church circa 1915 and the interior of the church in the 1940s and today. www.sacredheartflorissant.org

Old St. Ferdinand Shrine

The oldest Catholic congregation in St. Louis, founded in 1770. The Shrine is at the site of the earliest European settlements west of the Mississippi. The convent was built in 1819 and the first church in 1820. In 1959 the Friends of Old St. Ferdinand Shrine was formed to save the church and convent. It was designated a shrine in 1979 and placed on the National Register of Historic Places. The Friends of Old St. Ferdinand Inc. purchased the Shrine complex and continue to preserve it today. Visitors are welcome to visit the Shrine.
www.oldstferdinandshrine.com

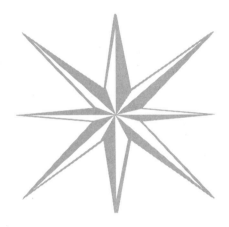

X. PAPERBACK WRITER

About the Authors

BILL KASALKO

After graduating from Labouré, Bill went on to St. Louis University, graduated in 1968, and later received his MA from Webster University. He and his wife Jan married in 1970 and have two sons, Jeff and David. He retired after 38 years in the insurance industry. He came to know Craig Kaintz when both worked at an employee benefits firm in 1980. At this time they realized they grew up on the same street in Bellefontaine Neighbors. They have remained friends since then and co-authored Cruizin' North County, published in 2008. They have teamed up again to write a new book with more North County memories, *Let's Go Cruizin' Again!*

CRAIG KAINTZ

Craig grew up in North City (St. Engelbert's Parish) and moved to North County (Our Lady of Good Counsel - OLGC) in Bellefontaine Neighbors in 1964. He met Rose in seventh grade at OLGC. Following Augustinian Academy, Craig attended St. Louis University, graduated in 1974, and then joined General American Life Insurance Company. Rose and Craig were married in 1976 at OLGC and have three children, Lauren, Christopher and Brendyn. Craig retired from Towers Watson in 2010 where he was the managing principal of the St. Louis office.

XI. R-E-S-P-E-C-T

Acknowledgements and Photo Credits

Aaron Hoffman – Hazelwood School District

Ann and Tom Towey – Prep North High School

Barbara and John McGuinness – Velvet Freeze

Bill Biermann – Ritenour High School

Bob Kaintz

Carmen Lombardo – Lombardo's Restaurant

Carmen Mannino – Mannino's Market

Charles Bolinger – Hazelwood School District

Charles E. Brown – St. Louis Globe Democrat Archives of the St. Louis
Mercantile Library at the University of Missouri-St. Louis

• Olympic Drive-In

• Totes

• 94th Aero Squadron

• Village Square Shopping Center

• Normandy Basketball Tournament

• Badenfest

• Spanish Lake Cinema

• Normandy Shopping Center

Chris Cusamano – Cusamano's

Chris Obermeier – Ritenour High School

Chris and Kathy Helfer – Helfer's Bakery and Deli Café

Chuck Rolwes – High school mascots, Johnny Mac's/North County

Cindy Gibson – Ritenour School District

Dan Dillon – So Where'd You Go to High School? Baby Boomer Edition;
Virginia Publishing Company

• High school stories and pictures

Dan Duncan – Castaway Club

Dan Grummich – Trinity Catholic High School

Dan LaRocca – LaRocca's Restaurant

Dan Reardon – St. Thomas Aquinas High School, Trinity Catholic High School

Dana Sabastian-Duncan – Ferguson Department Store, Northern Arts Council

Dave Grone – Grone's Cafeteria

David Henderson – McCluer High School

David Naumann – David L. Naumann, Attorneys at Law

Debbie and Ed Mueller – White Barn

Diana Gulotta – Hazelwood School District

Diana Niemeyer

Dick Fisher – Fischer's

Don Fitzpatrick

Don McElroy – 7th Street Meat Market

Dorman Pentecost – Chicken King

Doug Garner – Images of America, Forest Park Highlands;
Acadia Publishing

• Holiday Hill

• Westlake Amusement Park

• Chain of Rocks Amusement Park

Ellen and Kevin O'Sullivan – Normandy High School photos,
O'Sullivan-Muckle Mortuary

Eric Koppitz – Pine Lawn Steak 'n Shake, American Roadhouse Car Club

Fran Russo – Green Lea, Russo's Catering and Spazio's

Gary Crump – Paul's Market

Greg Campbell – Crest Bowl

Gretchen Crank; Rosemary Davison – Florissant Historical Society

• Sacred Heart

• Valley of the Flowers

• Burcke's

• Dirty Nellie's

Hank Darabsek – Farmers Club, Mississippi Valley Roofing Company

Heath Randall – Kiddie Land Amusement Park

Helen and Gary Nelling – Normandy High School

Jan and Jack Yacovelli – Yacovelli's Restaurant

Janice Buenger – Roberto's Italian Restaurant

Jane Byers – Riverview Gardens High School

Janet Dalton Campbell – Kinloch High School

Jeanne and Mike Nagle – Nagles, Ben Franklin and Holy Cross Children

Jeanne and Rich Rozycki – Rosary High School, 5 Star Travel '& Cruises'

Jeff Cook – BIGFOOT

Jeff Dintelman – Pattonville High School

Jessie Randazzo Nelke – Incarnate Word High School

Jim Grummich – Corpus Christi High School

Jim Healy – Golf Writer and Historian

• Glen Echo Country Club

• Norwood Hills Country Club

• Normandie Golf Club

• St. Vincent's Home for Children

Jan Kasalko

Jim Marshall – Faraci's Ferguson

Jim Miller

Joe Ann Croce – Wellston High School

Joe and Norma Milisitch – Corpus Christi High School

Joe Schulte – St. Ferdinand Shrine

John Meglio – Luigi's and Meglio's Italian Bar and Grill

Juanita Weber – Dick Weber Lanes

Judy Behrens Cuthbertson – Fairview High School

Keith Took – Old Town Donuts

Kelly Kendall – Pattonville School District

Linda Greiner – V.P. American Roadhouse Car Club

Linda Hack – Hazelwood East

Linda Schmerber – Jennings Historical Society

• Jennings Bulldog

• Fairview Blue Jay

• Janet Theater

• Jennings children

• Fairview/Jennings student picture

Lonnie Tettaton – St. Louis memories

• Chuck-A-Burger

Louise Overbey – Wellston High School

Maggie and Betty Vitale – Old Topper, Leprechaun Gold Bar

Mark Mispagel

Mark Russo – Green Lea, Russo's Catering and Spazio's

Mark Toenjes – Prep North

Mark Towey – Prep North

Matt Mcvey – McCluer North High School

Matthew Fog – Hodges Skating Rink

Mike Flanagan – Crest Bowl

Mike Hales – Ritenour High School

Nathan Bennett – Hendel's Restaurant

Nina and David Cissell – Incarnate Word High School

Nita Koen – Castaway Club

Norman Plant – 270 Drive-In

Oliver Dillingham – Kinloch High School

Pam and Peter Rosciglione – Rosciglione's Bakery

Pat Howley – Chain of Rocks Amusement Park and the Admiral

Paula Schneider – Pattonville High School

Peggy Gettemeier – Bergans Dairy

Peggy McVey – Glasgow Village

Rachael – Ruiz Mexican Restaurant

Randy Keeven – Doozle's Custard

Renee Shea – Glasgow Village

Rick Puckett – Pirrone's Pizzeria

Robin Dees – Ferguson-Florissant School District

Ron Davis – Ritenour High School

Ron Grubbs – Ritenour High School

Rose, Lauren, Christoper and Brendyn Kaintz

Russ Britton – Ole Topper, New Image Barber Shop

Russ Signorino – Rosary High School

Ruth Brown - Ferguson Historical Society, Ferguson, A City Remembered

• January Walbash Park

• Ferguson High School

• Downtown Ferguson

• Ferguson Bowl

• Savoy Theater

• Ferguson police cruizer

• Ferguson children

Shannon Howard – Editor/Publisher NOCOstl.com

Shantana Stewart – Ferguson-Florissant School District

Sharon (Sebbon) Wiemeier – Hodges Skating Rink

Sister Eileen O'Keefe – Incarnate Word High School

Steve Gruenwald – Lutheran North High School

Steve Hallemann – Glen Echo Country Club

Susan G Holtzman – Jennings High School

Taz Kirk – Ritenour High Schol

Terry and Debbie Wolf – Lutheran North High School

Tim Davidson – City of Hazelwood

Tom Hartnett – Ferguson

Tom Lauman

Tom Zak – City of Dellwood

Tony Valenti – Valenti's

Vito Saullo – Saullo's Pizzeria